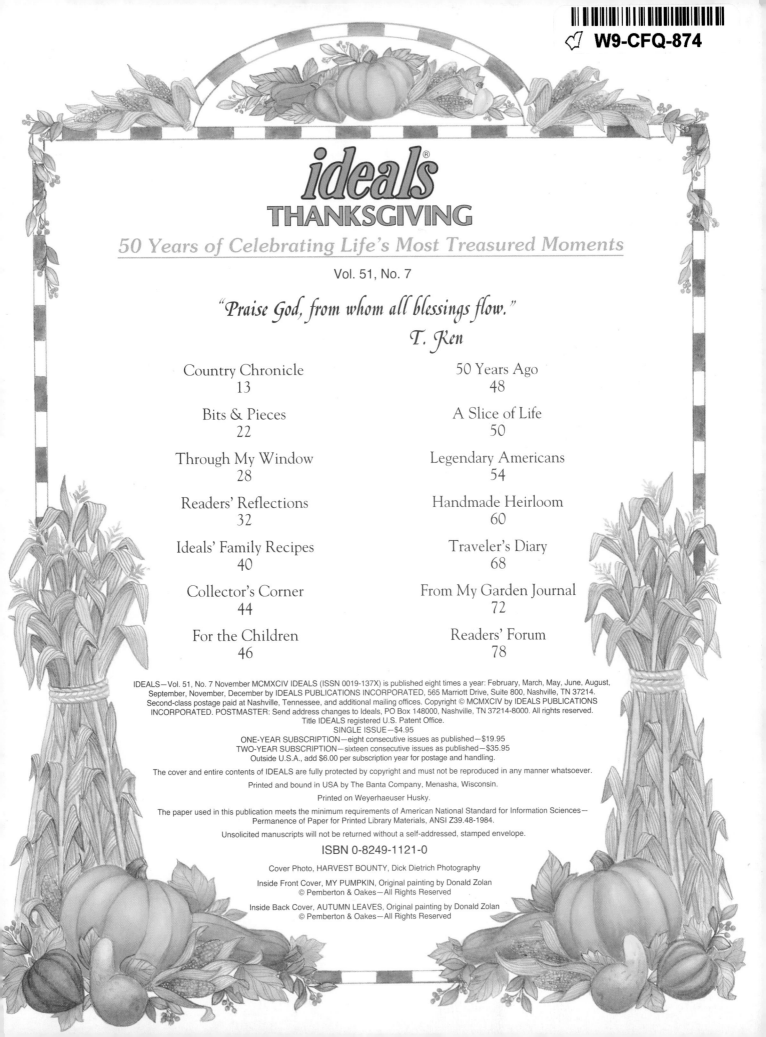

W9-CFQ-874

ideals®
THANKSGIVING

50 Years of Celebrating Life's Most Treasured Moments

Vol. 51, No. 7

"Praise God, from whom all blessings flow."

T. Ken

IDEALS—Vol. 51, No. 7 November MCMXCIV IDEALS (ISSN 0019-137X) is published eight times a year: February, March, May, June, August, September, November, December by IDEALS PUBLICATIONS INCORPORATED, 565 Marriott Drive, Suite 800, Nashville, TN 37214. Second-class postage paid at Nashville, Tennessee, and additional mailing offices. Copyright © MCMXCIV by IDEALS PUBLICATIONS INCORPORATED. POSTMASTER: Send address changes to Ideals, PO Box 148000, Nashville, TN 37214-8000. All rights reserved. Title IDEALS registered U.S. Patent Office.

SINGLE ISSUE—$4.95

ONE-YEAR SUBSCRIPTION—eight consecutive issues as published—$19.95
TWO-YEAR SUBSCRIPTION—sixteen consecutive issues as published—$35.95
Outside U.S.A., add $6.00 per subscription year for postage and handling.

Printed and bound in USA by The Banta Company, Menasha, Wisconsin.

Printed on Weyerhaeuser Husky.

The paper used in this publication meets the minimum requirements of American National Standard for Information Sciences—Permanence of Paper for Printed Library Materials, ANSI Z39.48-1984.

Unsolicited manuscripts will not be returned without a self-addressed, stamped envelope.

ISBN 0-8249-1121-0

Nature's Fall Garden

Loise Pinkerton Fritz

The treetops are sun-touched
    Along country lanes
That wend through the meadows
    And woodland terrain.
The leaves are so beauteous
    With color aflame,
Since nature is singing
    Its autumn refrain.

Near fence rows grow sumacs
    All coned with bright red,
And bordering these beauties
    Are goldenrod beds.
Sun's rays touch the earth shades
    And highlight each hue
Of nature's fall garden
    As autumn skips through.

GLADE CREEK GRIST MILL
Babcock State Park
Clifftop, West Virginia
Josiah Davidson Scenic Photography

Autumn Tapestry

Patience Strong

Framed within the casement
Of my window I can see
The rich and varied colors
Of the autumn tapestry
Worked in glowing shades of red
And russet, mauve, and blue,
The garden in the foreground
And beyond, the rolling view—

Sunflowers blazing round the path
And dahlias bold and bright;
Beds of gay chrysanthemums,
Bronze, amber, rose, and white,
Massed against the mellow background
Of the distant scene,
Stretching to the far horizon,
Brown and gold and green;

Furrowed acres newly plowed,
The corn shocks, and the hay;
Orchards, stubbles, cottage roofs,
And churches old and gray;
Meadow pastures, willow-fringed,
Where flow the winding streams—
Lovely as a picture
In the tapestry of dreams.

CARP RIVER
Porcupine Mountains State Wilderness Park
Upper Peninsula, Michigan
Jeff Gnass Photography

Asters and Goldenrod

Helen Jackson

I know the lands are lit
With all the autumn blaze of goldenrod;
And everywhere the purple asters nod
And bend and wave and flit.

But when the names I hear,
I never picture how their pageant lies

Spread out in tender stateliness of guise,
The fairest of the year.

I only see one nook,
A wooded nook — half sun, half shade —
Where one I love his footsteps sudden stayed
And whispered, "Darling, look!"

6

Two oak leaves, vivid green,
Hung low among the ferns and parted wide
While purple aster stars, close side by side,
Like faces peered between,

Like maiden faces set
In vine-wreathed window, waiting shy and glad
For joys whose dim, mysterious promise had
But promise been, as yet.

And, like proud lovers bent
In regal courtesy, as kings might woo,
Tall goldenrod, bareheaded in the dew,
Above the asters leant.

Ah, me! Lands will be lit
With every autumn's blaze of goldenrod;
And purple asters everywhere will nod
And bend and wave and flit

Until, like ripened seed,
This little earth itself, some noon, shall float
Off into space, a tiny shining mote,
Which none but God will heed.

But never more will be
Sweet asters peering through that branch of oak
To hear such precious words as dear lips spoke
That sunny day to me.

LACY GOLDENROD
Solidago "Peter Pan"
R. Todd Davis Photography

Our Thanksgiving

Marian L. Moore

When the golden leaves of autumn
    Lie rejected on the ground
And the heavy hand of winter
    Closes in on all around;

When the flowers of the summer
    Have all vanished with the frost
And the harvest of the season
    Has been gathered against loss;

As the geese wing slowly southward
    Where the warmer regions lie
And the year is swiftly ebbing
    With the moments as they fly;

Then the autumn brings Thanksgiving
    To our God for all His love.
For His care and many blessings,
    We shall lift our eyes above.

As the hymns of praise and thank you
    Fall upon each listening ear,
Let us offer true thanksgiving
    To our God all through the year!

HARVEST TIME

Marianna Jo Arolin

I welcome these crisp autumn days,
This abundant harvest time
When boughs are bent with apples
And pumpkins cling to vines,

The taste of hot, mulled cider,
Pungent wood smoke in the sky
That flows like long gray ribbons
From chimneys reaching high.

The last bright leaves have fallen.
Now hills are crimson-gold.
I watch breathtaking splendor
As harvest time unfolds.

HARVEST FIELD

Gertrude Ryder Bennett

The cornfield has its hair on end
    As if afraid of ghosts tonight.
Along the stubble, pumpkin suns
    Reflect last rays of autumn light.

A groundhog waddles into his hole,
    Its entrance dry and summer worn.
Startled, a rabbit with button tail
    Whisks behind a shock of corn.

And post rail dining, one gray squirrel
    Removes fat kernels from a husk
While time-defying hills beyond
    Are brushed away by feathered dusk.

Country CHRONICLE

Lansing Christman

During this season of reflection, it is natural that our thoughts go back to the Pilgrims and their first Thanksgiving at Plymouth Colony. On that day long ago they gathered to express their profound thanks to God for His providence. Their new land had yielded sustenance to give them succor and strength and life.

I like to think all of us are Pilgrims in a sense, for we too express our gratitude on our pilgrimage through the years. For the young, it is just beginning. For we who are octogenarians, it has been a long pilgrimage, one of trust and faith, of hope and love.

My own pilgrimage has been spent in the country, both in the state of New York and the state of South Carolina. Even when I was occupied in an office in the city, I continued to live with the hills I loved around me. There was the land—the woodlands and pastures and open fields. And I am still living among the hills. Here I greet the seasons as they come. Here I welcome the songs of birds and the loveliness of blossoms, not only in the dooryard flower beds but also in the woods and meadows, in the thickets and marshes. They are a part of my being, a part of my long pilgrimage through life.

To me, each day is a day of thanksgiving, a day of expressing my gratitude for the loveliness of the out-of-doors. Throughout the year, I wait for the sounds of the birds. The bluebird comes with its liquid, warbled song, the robins with their carols. The thrushes come with their carillon of bells, the cardinals with their whistles, and the doves with their coos. In spring, the blossoms come—the snowdrops and lilacs, the jonquils and lilies, the tulips and roses. Yet none is more important to me than the common dandelion.

I greet the dawn each morning and the sunsets each evening. I greet the rains and snows and ice. Spring comes along with its thaw and sends the brooks and streams into song. I accept icy chill of winter and stifling heat of summer as a part of my life in a countryside that gives me peace and tranquility.

All these are a part of my pilgrimage, and I go on through life giving thanks to God for the wonders of creation and His goodness to humankind.

The author of two published books, Lansing Christman has been contributing to Ideals *for over twenty years. Mr. Christman has also been published in several American, foreign, and braille anthologies. He lives in rural South Carolina.*

Mountain Music

Elizabeth McFerren Youtz

I love that mountain music
And the stomping of the feet
While in and out we're winding
To that good old fiddle beat.

Bright skirts in twirling colors
And gay ribbons bob and dip.
As we clasp our hands and circle,
Under arching arms we slip.

The jugman is a'oomping,
The bass-man slaps and thumps,
And the fiddler plays sweet music
While the dancers slide and jump.

We do-si-do together
As we circle left and right,
And the laughter of the dancers
Makes a joyous sound all night.

There's cider on the tables,
And there's plenty more to eat.
Long benches stand in waiting
For the ones with weary feet.

When the caller's voice grows husky
And the fiddler's job is done,
We'll sit around and marvel
At that mountain-music fun!

The Husking Bee

Phyllis C. Michael

When frost was on the pumpkin
And the birds had flown away,
'Twas time again for husking,
And you'd hear my father say,

"I'll get that corn in, Mother,
So as we can have a bee."
She'd answer, "Why yes, Father.
Any night's all right with me."

The corn shocks filled the barn floor;
There were lanterns hanging high.
We hurried with the milking;
Folks would soon be dropping by.

Then the sturdy rafters echoed
With their laughter and their song;
And the hours of work went quickly;
They were never very long.

I remember, I remember.
Oh, how well I see it all.
I was then a lad of twenty,
Brown of face and straight and tall.

I was husking with the others
When I shouted, "Look, red ear!"
And I held it high, then higher,
Though my knees felt kind of queer.

Every face turned toward Miss Sally—
Oh, to see her smile and blush.
She's the fairest at the party;
You could almost hear folks hush.

I bravely claimed TWO kisses.
What a happy pair we made!
As right there at that husking,
Springtime wedding plans were made.

Thanksgiving

May Allread Baker

Now when the sky is gray and overcast
And wild geese call with their loud, haunting cry,
When all the harvest's gathered in at last
And signs portend the coming winter nigh,

We thank Thee, Lord, for this, Your gift of grain
Drawn from the storehouse of the good, dark soil,
Fruits of the summer sun and summer rain,
Well-earned reward of healthy, honest toil.

For this, our land of freedom, long ago
Our brave forefathers left their native sod.
And when the crops were gathered and the snow
Of winter fell, they gave their thanks to God.

And so, down through the years, shall we again
For this rich heritage give thanks. Amen!

Thank You for the Sunsets

Lorraine Pintus

When I look at a newborn baby or see a majestic rainbow arched over a freshly washed landscape, my first impulse is to jump up and down like a high school cheerleader and yell "hooray!" But the onset of gray hairs encourages a more dignified reaction. So instead, I simply smile.

The cheerleader in me nearly escaped one evening as I was sitting on the beach watching the sun set. Awestruck, I marveled at the living painting before me. A canvas of blue sky stretched across the earth. Wispy, pink feathers danced playfully around a massive, orange sun. Sea gulls cried overhead, lifting a wing of farewell to their warm friend. As if embarrassed by lingering too long, the sun blushed and hastily retreated into the cold ocean. The sea opened its arms and pulled the sun down as God dipped His paintbrush in fire and set the sky aflame with glorious crimson banners.

It was an eternal moment. And suddenly it was over. The ocean flopped a tired wave onto the sandy beach. The sky sighed a lonely breath of wind. Dusk soaked up the last bit of sunlight.

A few sunburnt stragglers sauntered off as if nothing out of the ordinary had happened.

"Wait a minute!" I shouted at them in my mind. "Didn't you see that sunset? Have you ever seen such splendor? Shouldn't we tell God 'thank you'?"

I wanted to shake my joy into them; to run up and down the beach and yell "Yea God!"; to turn cartwheels in the sand; to laugh and dance and sing. But I sat there, immobilized by inhibitions, afraid to make a fool of myself. Yet King David wasn't afraid of looking foolish. He danced before the Israelites in an outpouring of praise to God (2 Samuel 6:14).

Maybe I'd do things differently if I could turn back the clock.

I imagined myself sitting on the sand just before sunset. As the firey colors spread through the sky, I stood and began to applaud.

"Thank you, God!" I shouted.

A couple nearby stared in disapproval.

A teenager sipped a soda and watched me thoughtfully. Then she nodded in my direction, punched the sky with her fist, and yelled "awesome!"

Two children dropped their sand pails and sang "God is so good."

A golden retriever yipped in delight. Sea gulls cried out in happiness. And one by one, people began to join me in my standing ovation, clapping boldly and loudly.

Back in the present, all was quiet. The beach was empty except for an old man with a cane plodding a path through the sand a few yards from me. His lips curled upward in a toothless grin. "Enjoy the sunset?"

Resisting the urge to grab his cane and lead the heavenly band strutting in my heart, I smiled and said "wonderful."

As he shuffled by, he looked straight at me and winked. Suddenly I knew! Here was another of God's cheerleaders! We shared a moment of silent communion. His eyes reassured me that throughout the sunset God had listened to our unspoken praise.

The old man turned and hobbled away. In my mind, I saw him stop, lay down his cane, and turn a cartwheel in the sand.

My Daily Prayer

Kay Hoffman

Give me a spirit sweet, dear Lord,
　　As I go about my day,
That I would be a blessing glad
　　To someone on life's way.

Let no small pettiness of mine
　　Keep me from doing good,
To help where there's a need and love
　　My neighbor as I should.

When I would seek my will, not Yours,
　　Speak to my heart anew;
Give me a vision clear, dear Lord,
　　Of what You'd have me do.

Please grant to me the strength I need
　　To stand for right and good,
Rememb'ring that we all should strive
　　To do the things You would.

Lord, let me not be boastful of
　　Some good that I have done,
But keep me ever mindful that
　　From You my blessings come.

I do not ask for riches grand,
　　Nor skies forever fair;
A closer walk with You, dear Lord,
　　This is my daily prayer.

NEW ENGLAND MEETING HOUSE
Village of Strafford, Vermont
Jeff Gnass Photography

BITS & PIECES

O Lord! that lends me life,
Lend me a heart replete with thankfulness!
Shakespeare, Henry VI

Gratitude is the heart's memory.
French Proverb

A thankful heart is the parent of all virtues.
Cicero

Our blessings are what we have by purchase;
and the purchase is made of God.
Jonathan Edwards

Blessed is he that always judges himself and
condemns himself and not another.
St. Francis

O give thanks unto the Lord; call upon his name:
make known his deeds among the people.
Psalms 105:1

Bless to us the pleasures, bless to us the pains
of our existence. Watch upon our eyes, ears,
thoughts, tongues, and hands that we may not think
unkindly, speak unwisely, nor act unrighteously.
Robert Louis Stevenson

Thanksgiving Day is only our annual time
for saying grace at the table of eternal goodness.
James M. Ludlow

Once more, my soul, the rising day
Salutes thy waking eyes;
Once more, my voice, thy tribute pay
To Him who rules the skies.
Isaac Watts

Gratitude is the sign of noble souls.
Aesop

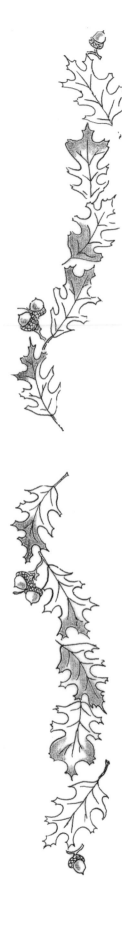

THE FIRST THANKSGIVING. Original painting by Jennie Augusta Brownscombe (1850-1936). Superstock, Inc.

THE FIRST THANKSGIVING DAY

Florence Ray

A very long, long time ago
  In England far away
Were Pilgrim folks who thought it wise
  To leave their homes one day,
That they might find another land
  Where free they all would be
To build a church of their own choice
  And worship peacefully.

To freedom, then, across the sea
  And westward many a week
They sailed the sturdy *Mayflower*
  In weather rough and bleak.
The voyage was a dreary one,
  The days were long and gray,
And restless children on the ship
  Found little room to play.

24

At last the Pilgrims sighted land.
    America they found,
Where they could live and worship God
    Upon that precious ground.
With homes to build and fields to plow
    Their plans were swiftly laid.
It was not very long before
    A village they had made.

The colored leaves began to fall;
    The ducks and geese flew high;
The setting sun hung red and low
    Along the western sky.
While autumn's rich and mellow days
    Were at their very best,
The Pilgrims then proclaimed a day
    To worship, feast, and rest.

Oh, what a bustle! What a stir!
    To plan the feast and bake
The puddings, pies, and loaves of bread,
    And even johnnycake,
To roast the turkeys and the deer,
    To bake the clams they found.
The air was filled with luscious smells
    From kitchens all around.

And then the Indian guests arrived
    To share the heaping trays;
Their fellowship was Heaven blest,
    And friends they all did stay.
The time to feast had come at last
    And then a time for play,
All underneath the autumn sun
    That first Thanksgiving day.

from The Song of Hiawatha

Henry Wadsworth Longfellow

By the shores of Gitche Gumee,
By the shining Big-Sea-Water,
Stood the wigwam of Nokomis,
Daughter of the Moon, Nokomis.
Dark behind it rose the forest,
Rose the black and gloomy pine trees,
Rose the firs with cones upon them;
Bright before it beat the water,
Beat the clear and sunny water,
Beat the shining Big-Sea-Water.
There the wrinkled, old Nokomis
Nursed the little Hiawatha,
Rocked him in his linden cradle,
Bedded soft in moss and rushes,
Safely bound with reindeer sinews.

INDIAN ENCAMPMENT
Original painting by Martin Mower
Fine Art Photographic Library Ltd.

THROUGH MY WINDOW

Pamela Kennedy

Art by Russ Flint

THE QUILT

"Mom, don't we have any Thanksgiving decorations?" my daughter yelled as she burst in from school, out of breath from her dash home in the chilly November drizzle. "We're supposed to decorate our classrooms for Thanksgiving, and the room with the best decorations gets a prize. Don't we have anything I can take?"

"I'm right in the middle of something. Can it wait a few minutes?" I answered. It rarely occurs to my daughter that there is life outside of her eleven-year-old world. When I finished, I found her in the family room rifling through a chest of drawers that has become the family repository for junk too good to part with.

"That's not where I keep the decorations.

28

Come in here," I said and led her to an antique trunk in the living room. Carefully removing the plant and lamp the trunk supported, I unlatched it and pushed back the heavy lid.

"Look at all this neat stuff!" my daughter exclaimed. She began removing valentine hearts and St. Patrick's Day shamrocks, scattering red and green glitter on the rug. "I didn't know we had all this!" she said.

"I know," I replied with a grin. "That's why we still have it."

"Oh, Mom, I'll be careful," she promised. "This is really great." She carefully draped a garland of tiny Halloween pumpkins around her neck and adjusted a New Year's crown on her head. "Where'd we get all this?"

"Well, some of it is from my family, and some is from Dad's. I just don't use it much because it is sort of sentimental." I rummaged around until I found a large fold-out turkey and a couple of paper pilgrims. "If you promise to be careful with them, you can take these to school. When I was little, Grandma always used to put these on the table at Thanksgiving when the aunts and uncles and cousins came for dinner."

"Oh, they're perfect!" She reverently placed them on the rug.

"They won't break," I said, laughing at her awe.

"But they're practically antiques!"

I poked her gently in the ribs. "Not quite."

"What's in the big box at the bottom?"

I looked into the trunk and spied the edge of a battered, red coat box. "Oh, haven't I ever shown you that? Here, help me get it."

Together we removed the things on top of the box and then lifted it out. After opening it, my daughter folded back the layers of tissue paper. Her eyes widened when she saw the quilt.

"Oh, Mom, it's beautiful!" she exclaimed. "Where did you get it?"

"Well, when Grandma was waiting for me to be born, she made the squares. It was going to be a sunbonnet girl quilt for me when I was a baby." I pointed out how each square featured a little girl made of calico prints and solids. "I'm not sure why she didn't finish it. Anyway, after I was married, I found all the squares in an old chest and asked her if I could have them. When I was pregnant with your brother, I put the squares together into a baby quilt; but then when he turned out to be a boy, I didn't think it was very appropriate, so I tucked it away. I guess I just forgot about it."

She traced the black outline stitch around one of the sunbonnet girls. In one of those flashes of "mother insight," I sensed her thoughts.

"You know," I said, stroking her long hair, "I think you're old enough to take good care of this now. Would you like to keep it on your bed?"

"Really?" Her eyes sparkled with delight. "It will remind me of Grammy and you and me—all of the women in our family put together; and when I'm in bed at night, it will be like having a hug around me all the time! Thanks, Mom. This is the best gift ever!" She gathered up the quilt and the paper decorations and ran upstairs to her room.

As I sat there placing the faded decorations back in the trunk, I thought about what my daughter had said. She was right. The generations of a family, the memories, the little bits of memorabilia that bind us to each other are like a hug that spans the years. Selfishly, I had tucked so many of them away, not wanting them to be damaged. But in doing so I had kept their comforting warmth from others. This Thanksgiving, I had accidentally discovered more than an old quilt. I had found in the wisdom of my child a wonderful legacy for which to be thankful.

Pamela Kennedy is a free-lance writer of short stories, articles, essays, and children's books. Wife of a naval officer and mother of three children, she has made her home on both U.S. coasts and currently resides in Honolulu, Hawaii. She draws her material from her own experiences and memories, adding bits of her imagination to create a story or mood.

Thoughts of Thankfulness

John C. Bonser

For happy times of joy and mirth,
For harvest riches from the earth,
For challenges that test our worth—
We thank you, Lord, for all of these.

For nursery songs a mother sings,
For fireflies and bluebirds' wings,
For all life's gentle, little things—
We thank you, Lord, for such as these.

For peace that sheathes the warrior's sword,
For noble deed and kindly word,
For lands where freedom's voice is heard—
We thank you, Lord; grant these increase!

For home and hearth where we can rest
Among the dear ones we know best,
For all good things whereby we're blessed—
We thank you, Lord, for gifts like these.

For every church and holy place
Where we may come to seek your grace
And know that no one's rank or race
Will cause your love for us to cease,

We thank you, Lord, and pray that we
May closer grow in harmony
Till goodwill clothes humanity
In robes of kindness, love, and peace!

30

HILLSBORO CENTER CHURCH
New Hampshire
Gene Ahrens Photography

Readers' Reflections

Editor's Note: Readers are invited to submit unpublished, original poetry for possible publication in future issues of Ideals. Please send copies only; manuscripts will not be returned. Writers receive $10 for each published submission. Send material to "Readers' Reflections," Ideals Publications Inc., P.O. Box 148000, Nashville, TN 37214-8000.

Thanksgiving

Dear Lord, on this Thanksgiving Day
With grateful hearts we bow and pray
For blessings given from our birth
Exceeding way beyond our worth—
For friends who've proven to be true;
For pets, which count as friendships too;
For home and country, health and love—
All sent to us from Heaven above.
Lord, please continue to be near
And guide us through another year.

Carol Neumann
Jersey City, New Jersey

Speak to me of God

A flower, a plant,
    a tiny ant,
Speak to me of God.

A smile, a child,
    flowers wild,
Speak to me of God.

The sun above,
    your words of love,
Speak to me of God.

May I, in turn,
    with thanks return
Speak to thee of God.

Sister Eleanor Easly
Scottdale, Pennsylvania

Thanksgiving Prayer

With thankful hearts we praise You, Lord,
    On this Thanksgiving Day.
We ask that You stay near us
    And hear us as we pray.

For food and shelter we are grateful,
    For all the blessings from above,
For health, for friends, for dear one
    For showing us Your love.

We're grateful for the rain You send
    And for the sunshine bright and warm,
For all the times You've kept from us
    Misfortune, grief, and harm.

The greatest gift of all, though, Lord,
    Is Jesus Christ, Your Son,
Who is our loving Saviour
    And a friend to everyone.

Kathleen Boehm
Kansas City, Missouri

The Nightingale

Once I saw a nightingale
    Perched upon a limb.
I listened for a moment,
    And then I spoke to him.

How can you sing so prettily,
    And fill the air with song
When all the world is upside down
    And so many things are wrong?

He warbled out another tune
    And then spread his wings in flight.
I suddenly felt a glow of peace,
    And all the world seemed right.

If only we, like the nightingale,
    Would raise our voice in song
Throughout the world in harmony,
    How could anything go wrong?

Kathleen Lowery
Frankston, Texas

We Give Thanks

George Z. Keller

Great Author of the harvest time
And Master of us all,
We pause this blest Thanksgiving Day,
Thy blessings to recall.

Thy benefactions fill the air
    And bless in countless ways
The righteous and the erring ones
    Who tread life's puzzling maze.

Thy mercy drops as gentle rain
    On parched and barren soil,
Bestowing Thy refreshing grace
    On all who rest or toil.

Oh, those there are who fail to see
    Behind life's shifting scenes
The Hand that guides by night and day
    And what such guidance means.

Forgive us for our past offense
    And lead us in the way
As we acknowledge all Thy gifts
    On this Thanksgiving Day.

Fall Sparrows

Angela Gall

The cold, late autumn weather seemed
No time for nesting; but the pair,
We guessed, had spied this place, deemed
Just right—our spacious hanging basket
Of pink geraniums with one bloom.
The basket swayed, and plans took shape
As grasses, twigs, and bright pink plume
Circled to cradle baby ones.
We applauded the chirping, gritty
Two on their finished, arduous work—
Sturdy, cat-safe, and flower pretty.

Nutting

Mary Russell Mitford

The harvest is nearly over, the fields are deserted, the silence may almost be felt. Except the wintry notes of the redbreast, Nature herself is mute. But how beautiful, how gentle, how harmonious, how rich! The rain has preserved to the herbage all the freshness and verdure of spring; and the world of leaves has lost nothing of its midsummer brightness; and the harebell is on the banks; and the woodbine in the hedges; and the low furze, which the lambs cropped in the spring, has burst again into its golden blossoms.

All is beautiful that the eye can see, perhaps the more beautiful for being shut in with a forest-like closeness. We have no prospect in this labyrinth of lanes, crossroads, mere cartways, leading to the innumerable little farms into which this part of the parish is divided. Uphill or down, these quiet, wooly lanes scarcely give us a peep at the world except when, leaning over a gate, we look into one of the small enclosures, hemmed in with hedgerows, so closely set with growing timber that the meady openings look almost like a glade in a wood; or when some cottage, planted at a corner of one of the little greens formed by the meeting of these crossways, almost startles us by the unexpected sight of the dwellings of men in such solitude. . . . Even this pretty, snug farmhouse on the hillside, with its front covered with the rich vine, which goes wreathing up to the very top of the clustered chimney, and its sloping orchard full of fruit—even this pretty, quiet nest can hardly peep out of its leaves. Ah! They are gathering in the orchard harvest. Look at that young rogue in the old, mossy apple tree—that great tree, bending with the weight of its golden fruit—see how he pelts his little sister beneath with apples as red and as round as her own cheeks, while she, with her outstretched frock, is trying to catch them and laughing and offering to pelt again as often as one bobs against her. . . .

Then farther up the orchard that bold, hardy lad, the eldest-born, who has scaled (Heaven knows how!) the tall, straight, upper branch of that great pear tree and is sitting there as securely and as fearlessly, in as much real safety and apparent danger, as a sailor on the topmast. Now he shakes the tree with a mighty swing that brings down a pelting shower of stony bergamots, which the father gathers rapidly up whilst the mother can hardly assist for her motherly fear—a fear which only spurs the spirited boy to bolder ventures. . . .

The little spring that has been bubbling under the hedge all along the hillside begins, now that we have mounted the eminence and are imperceptibly descending, to deviate into a capricious variety of clear, deep pools and channels, so narrow and so choked with weeds that a child might overstep them. . . . "Ah, there are still nuts on that bough!" and in an instant my dear companion, active and eager and delighted as a boy, has hooked down with his walking stick one of the lissome hazel stalks and cleared it of its tawny clusters; and in another moment he has mounted the bank and is in the midst of the nuttery, now transferring the spoil from the lower branches into that vast variety of pockets which gentlemen carry about them, now bending the tall tops into the lane, holding them down by main force, so that I might reach them and enjoy the pleasure of collecting some of the plunder myself. . . .

So on we go, scrambling and gathering with all our might and all our glee. Oh, what an enjoyment! All my life long I have had a passion for that sort of seeking which implies finding (the secret, I believe, of the love of field sports, which is in man's mind a natural impulse)—therefore, I love violeting; therefore, when we had a fine garden, I used to love to gather strawberries and cut asparagus and, above all, to collect the filberts from the shrubberies; but this hedgerow nutting beats that sport all to nothing.

Favorite Recipes from the Ideals Family of Readers

Editor's Note: If you'd like us to consider your favorite recipe, please send a typed copy of the recipe along with your name, address, and phone number to Ideals magazine, ATTN: Recipes, P.O. Box 148000, Nashville, Tennessee 37214-8000. We will pay $10 for each recipe used. Recipes cannot be returned.

CRANBERRY-APPLE MINI LOAVES

In a small mixing bowl, stir together ½ cup whole cranberry sauce, ½ cup chopped nuts, and ½ teaspoon finely shredded orange peel; set aside.

In a medium mixing bowl, stir together 1½ cups flour, 1 cup granulated sugar, 1 teaspoon ground cinnamon, ½ teaspoon baking soda, ¼ teaspoon salt, ¼ teaspoon baking powder, and ¼ teaspoon ground allspice. Make a well in center of dry mixture.

In another medium mixing bowl, combine 1 egg, beaten, ½ cup finely shredded, peeled apple, and ¼ cup cooking oil; mix well. Add apple mixture all at once to dry mixture and stir just until moistened (batter will be lumpy). Pour half of the batter into four greased 4½-x-2½-x-1½-inch loaf pans (about ⅓ cup batter per pan). Spoon about 2 tablespoons cranberry mixture on top of batter in each pan. Top each with remaining batter. Spoon remaining cranberry mixture down the center of each loaf. Bake loaves in a preheated 350° oven for 35 to 40 minutes or till done. Cool on wire rack 10 minutes. Remove loaves from pans.

In a small mixing bowl, stir together ½ cup powdered sugar, sifted, and enough orange juice (about 1 tablespoon) to make an icing of drizzling consistency. Drizzle over warm loaves.

Misty White
Arlington, Massachusetts

BANANA CRANBERRY CREAM PIE

In a medium mixing bowl, stir together one 16-ounce can whole cranberry sauce, 2 tablespoons lemon juice, and 1 teaspoon grated lemon rind. In a glass or metal bowl, sprinkle one envelope plain gelatin over ¼ cup cold water and let stand one minute; place bowl over a pan of boiling water and stir to dissolve gelatin. Stir gelatin into cranberry-sauce mixture. Chill until slightly thickened.

Peel and slice 2 ripe bananas. Fold lightly into cranberry-sauce mixture. Pour into 1 baked pastry shell and chill until firm. Top with 1 cup heavy cream, whipped, or whipped topping; if desired, garnish with banana slices dipped in lemon juice.

Ethyle Cutting
Greenhurst, New York

FROZEN CRANBERRY SALAD

In a large mixing bowl, stir together one 16-ounce can whole cranberry sauce, one 20-ounce can crushed pineapple, drained, and ½ cup chopped walnuts. In a separate mixing bowl, stir together one 14-ounce can sweetened condensed milk and ¼ cup lemon juice; add to cranberry-sauce mixture and stir well. Fold in one 10-ounce container whipped topping. Pour into a 9-x-13-x-2-inch pan and freeze until ready to serve.

Marie Bubb
Stockton, California

CECIL'S CRANBERRY SHERBET

In a large saucepan, combine 4 cups whole cranberries and 1½ cups water; boil until skin pops open on berries. Cool berries and run through sieve; retain pulp and discard the residue. In a medium mixing bowl, combine pulp, 2 cups granulated sugar, ½ cup orange juice, and 2 tablespoons lemon juice; stir well. Freeze mixture until it reaches a mushy consistency (close to two hours). In a separate bowl, beat 2 egg whites until soft peaks form. Add ½ pint heavy cream, whipped, and fold into cranberry mixture. Pour into a 9-x-13-x-2-inch pan and freeze until ready to serve; cut in squares to serve. Or freeze mixture in mixing bowl and scoop sherbet with small ice cream scoop to serve in sherbet glasses.

Carlee Hallman
Frederick, Maryland

Kneading Bread

Belle Banister Broadbent

While the dough I gently grasp,
I think of those who must clasp
Seed, to sow the golden grain
And reap the harvest it contains;
And those who then work hour by hour
Turning this grain into flour
While these joining, clasping hands
Feed the hungry of the lands.
So I find a kinship spread
While I'm gently kneading bread.

TURKEY DINNER
Jessie Walker Associates

COLLECTOR'S CORNER

Lisa C. Thompson

FIESTA. Photograph by Jessie Walker Associates.

FIESTA
Art Deco Dinnerware

Anyone who has taken pride in creating a beautiful table setting can appreciate the creative opportunities in Fiesta dinnerware, a many-hued, mix-and-match art deco line from the 1930s. The sleek design and seemingly endless color palette of Fiesta brings out the hidden artist in any collector and makes serving a simple grilled cheese sandwich almost as much fun as serving an elaborate, seven-course Thanksgiving dinner.

The gifted designer of the Fiesta line, Frederick Rhead, was born in Staffordshire, England, in 1880. A sixth-generation potter, Rhead apprenticed under his father following his studies at the Wedgwood Institute in Burslem and the Stoke-on-Trent Government Art School. When he emigrated to the United States in 1902, Rhead became more and more involved in and fascinated with commercial pottery. Fiesta was not the first line of dinnerware he designed, but it was by far the most successful. By the time he designed Fiesta, Rhead had learned the importance of analyzing his intended market carefully to determine the interests and buying power of the American people who would purchase his line. In his research, Rhead noticed an exciting trend in the importance of color in the production of automobiles and household appliances and decided to incorporate the trend in the design of his new dishes. He also wanted the dinnerware to have a fun, informal feel that wouldn't alienate the everyday buyer. Fiesta fit the bill and then some.

In 1935 Rhead designed Fiesta for the Homer Laughlin China Company, which then successfully marketed the dinnerware the next year despite the struggling Depression economy. Inexpensive and readily available, Fiesta was introduced on the low end of the market and sold in stores such as Woolworth's. This sleek, new design was a welcome addition on the tables of thousands of Americans across the country. While Fiesta was marketed to the lower classes, even the more well-to-do set found themselves cutting corners during the Depression and purchased the bright dinnerware enthusiastically. Fiesta sold millions. The success of the line was due in part to the strategic marketing of the Homer Laughlin China Company, but the key component was Rhead's elegant, modern pattern that effectively revolutionized American industrial design.

Fiesta is easily recognized by its bright colors, simple pattern of concentric rings, and, in some pieces, striking stick handles. When Rhead chose the original colors, he deliberated long and hard; they were not the result of mere artistic whim. Rhead specifically wanted bright colors that would contrast pointedly with one another and also look attractive in any combination on the table. He achieved his goal remarkably well with the original five colors of the line: yellow, green, ivory, cobalt blue, and "Fiesta red," which is really red-orange in appearance. Turquoise made its debut in 1938 and is often grouped with the original colors by collectors. Several years passed before the new 1950s color scheme was introduced, and Fiesta collectors eagerly added dark green, rose, chartreuse, and gray to their table settings. Medium green, the last color of the original Fiesta design, was presented in 1959 and was produced for only ten years. As a result, medium green is the rarest hue and therefore the most sought after by collectors.

In 1969 Fiesta was completely restyled and introduced in three colors: antique gold, mango red, and turf green. Just four years later, the entire line was discontinued. Happily, Fiesta was reissued in 1986 in commemoration of the dinnerware's fiftieth anniversary. The anniversary colors are black, white, rose, apricot, and dark blue.

Fiesta collectors scavenge through flea markets and garage sales as well as frequent pricier antique stores and art deco shops to procure their passion. The prices they pay for Fiesta pieces vary widely depending on the dish itself and also the color. The covered onion soup bowl, only issued between 1936 and 1938, is a coveted item among collectors. Any of the accessory items, such as tripod candlesticks or bud vases, will usually fetch higher prices than a simple dinner plate or mug. Also, fewer pieces were issued in the 1950s colors, which drives the price up on pieces in any of those hues.

Many Fiesta pieces include the "Fiesta" mark—the word in script either indented or stamped in ink. Some pieces of the line, such as the salt and pepper shakers, never included the "Fiesta" mark, while other pieces, including the highly-prized, covered onion soup bowl, were marked only occasionally.

Collectors are always looking for innovative ways in which to display their collectibles, and what better way for Fiesta collectors to share the beauty of their prized pieces than to set the table for Thanksgiving dinner in a virtual rainbow of color with Fiesta.

FOR THE CHILDREN
ARTWORK BY RUSS FLINT

COME, LITTLE LEAVES

George Cooper

"Come, little leaves," said the wind one day,
"Come o'er the meadows with me and play;
Put on your dresses of red and gold,
For summer is gone and the days grow cold."

Soon as the leaves heard the wind's loud call,
Down they came fluttering, one and all;
Over the brown fields they danced and flew,
Singing the glad little songs they knew.

"Cricket, goodbye, we've been friends so long;
Little brook, sing us your farewell song;
Say you are sorry to see us go;
Ah, you will miss us, right well we know.

"Dear little lambs in your fleecy fold,
Mother will keep you from harm and cold;
Fondly we watched you in vale and glade;
Say, will you dream of our loving shade?"

Dancing and whirling, the little leaves went;
Winter had called them, and they were content;
Soon, fast asleep in their earthy beds,
The snow laid a coverlid over their heads.

The unique perspective of Russ Flint's artistic style has made him a favorite of Ideals *readers for many years. A resident of California and father of four, Russ Flint has illustrated a children's Bible and many other books.*

QUIET TIME. Original painting by Donald Zolan. © Pemberton & Oakes—All Rights Reserved.

Two Hundred Years of Children's Books

Could all the characters in children's books that have followed in the John Newbery tradition gather to celebrate the two-century milestone since the appearance of his first little publication for the young, what a gay and interesting company they would be! We can picture the genial bookseller of St. Paul's Churchyard, London, welcoming the throng, astonished a bit, but inordinately proud, no doubt, to see how sturdy and varied that branch of English literature is that has grown from the venture he started as a side line—possibly more as a diversion than anything else.

It was a happy thought that children's books should entertain as well as instruct. The little books sold and sold well. Mr. Newbery reaped the immediate rewards that come from launching a popular venture and has earned the gratitude of children ever since for beginning their liberation from the didactic tale with the moral lesson as its first concern.

Mr. Newbery deserves our commendation too for approaching writing for children with respect, as worthy of the efforts of the best writers. His little books were published anonymously, but there are

48

reliable indications that many of them were by well-known authors.

The first of Mr. Newbery's books for children, whose bicentennial is celebrated this year [1944], was *A Little Pretty Pocket-Book Intended for the Instruction and Amusement of Little Master Tommy and Pretty Miss Polly.* Its publisher's ideas about books for children crossed the Atlantic thirty-three years later when an American edition was published by Isaiah Thomas at Worcester, Massachusetts, in 1787.

This engaging little volume, plentifully illustrated, contains, among many other entertaining features, two letters from Jack the Giant Killer, and "A Little Song Book, being a new attempt to teach children the use of the English alphabet by way of diversion." Compare the opening couplet of this alphabet with that of the *New England Primer*, published little more than half a century before, and you will recognize the value of Mr. Newbery's gift to childhood.

In Adam's fall
    We sinned all,

chants the *New England Primer*, but Mr. Newbery's "Little Song Book" introduces the alphabet with a hint of fun. Beneath a picture of children playing blindman's buff, with a blindfolded cat in the middle, runs the cheerful ditty:

Great A, B, and C,
    And tumble down D,
The Cat's a blind buff,
    And she cannot see.

With his insistence upon amusement, John Newbery made history in the field of children's books. The idea has been gaining strength and influence ever since. It is fascinating to trace the milestones of its growth through the eighteenth and nineteenth centuries to the present day. Today, the quality of story content and of illustration in many of the new books is so high that we look expectantly for them each season.

But there is one phase of current book publication for children which cannot be overlooked. It is the comic book. The comic book is not in the John Newbery tradition.

"The appeal of the comics is partly the result of social pressures," said Mrs. Frances Clarke Sayers, supervisor of work with children at the New York Public Library. "I've seen a boy come into the library with his pockets stuffed with comics and go out carrying Howard Pyle's *Robin Hood.* That doesn't worry me at all, because I know he has the taste to choose a good book when he has the chance.

"When a child reads only comics and nothing else, then is the time to be concerned. Then parents should step in and share the enjoyment of books with the child. They should explain to the child the difference in a motive and drive, between what is real and what is concocted. In reading a good book the child shares the creative experience of the author."

Miss Helen Dean Fish, well-known author and editor, and Mrs. Bertha Mahony Miller, editor of *The Horn Book*, also believe that the comics are defrauding children of their right to know good books.

Mrs. Miller said that when a child displayed a taste for comic books, his parents should counteract their influence by giving him plenty of good reading and cultivating his taste for good pictures. "Crowd the comics out with good books," she advised.

In the home of an eleven-year-old boy I know, there is no comic book problem. "Michael buys a comic book once in a while—perhaps four or five in a year," his mother said, seeming unaware of having done anything in particular to head the comics off. "He spends most of his reading time on the good books he has."

Curious to hear Michael's comment, I asked him whether he and his friends liked the comics.

"I don't read many comic books, but the kids I know read them a lot," he replied. "I think the kids read them because they haven't a chance at the good books, such as *Homer Price, The Jack Tales, Our Own USA,* and books about carpentry, much better than comics."

John Newbery would have an answer to the comic book. And, judging from his comments in his own little publications, he would say, "Take heed to what company you intrust your child."

Originally printed in The Christian Science Monitor Magazine, *November 11, 1944.*

A SLICE OF LIFE

Edgar A. Guest

Apples Ripe for Eating

Apples ripe for eating, and the grate fire blazing high,
And outside the moon of autumn fairly swimming in the sky,
The cellar packed with good things from the vine and field and tree—
Oh, the speech of man can't tell it, but it somehow seems to me
With such warmth and cheer around us, we should all burst into song
And store enough of gladness now to last our whole lives long.

Apples ripe for eating—there's a joy beyond compare
To pay for all our trouble and the burdens we must bear!
The bowl upon the table filled with round and rosy cheeks,
And enough down in the cellar to last all the winter weeks,
So that when the bowl is empty we can fill it up again—
And in spite of that we grumble and we bitterly complain.

I sometimes sit and wonder, as we pack life's fruits away
And hoard them in the cellar for the bleak and wintry day,
Why the mind of man has never tried to store a stock of cheer
In the cellar of his memory for the barren time of year
So that when joy's bowl is emptied and he thinks that life is vain,
He can seek his hoard of pleasures and just fill it up again.

Apples ripe for eating and a stock of them below
For the long cold nights of winter we shall shortly come to know,
So that when we need a pleasure that will seem to soothe the soul,
We can wander to the cellar and fill up the apple bowl;
So we could, if we were mindful, when our hearts with grief are sad,
Refresh our faltering courage with the pleasures we have had.

Edgar A. Guest began his illustrious career in 1895 at the age of fourteen when his work first appeared in the Detroit Free Press. *His column was syndicated in over 300 newspapers, and he became known as "The Poet of the People."*

November

Gladys Taber

THANKSGIVING is a very special holiday, for it is national, religious, and nonsectarian. It has, so far, escaped most of the commercialism that surrounds Christmas. And it is peculiarly a family holiday, a time for homecoming. I have always loved the exciting, wonderful Christmas celebration, although more and more I hear people saying they wish it were over because they are so tired.

But Thanksgiving does mean the giving of thanks to God, and it is a holiday belonging only to our country, reminding us of the Pilgrims who found a day in the midst of their battle for survival to praise God and ask for His blessing.

The traditional turkey has lost its grandeur since turkey is available any time of year. There isn't anything special about vegetables out of season either, for they are always in season along with fruit and mincemeat for pies. But the gathering of families around the table has the beauty of tradition on this day.

Nancy Skarmeas

John Chapman
Johnny Appleseed

In spring of the year 1800, residents of Steubenville, Ohio, witnessed an astonishing sight on the nearby Ohio River. Drifting downstream in a makeshift boat concocted from two canoes lashed together was an odd-looking man amidst a cargo of decaying apples. The man was barefoot, dressed in a cut-up coffee sack, and wearing a tin pan for a hat. That man was twenty-five-year-old John Chapman, who was a stranger to frontier America at the time but would become in the next fifty years a living legend known to all by the name of Johnny Appleseed.

Born in 1775 in either Boston or Springfield, Massachusetts, John Chapman was a man with a unique perspective on life and a unique self-appointed mission. Little is known about his life before 1800, but in that year stories first began to circulate among frontier settlers in Ohio of a man with a passion for apple trees and a disregard for all things material. Staying one step ahead of the expanding western frontier throughout Ohio and later Indiana, John Chapman earned the nickname of Johnny Appleseed by planting a series of tiny apple nurseries that he began with seeds collected from cider mills in Pennsylvania. He stayed long enough to nurture the young trees into saplings before he gave them away and moved on. When homesteaders began to arrive, Johnny Appleseed provided them with young apple saplings for their property, asking nothing in return except the planting and nurturing of his trees. Contrary to popular legend, Johnny Appleseed did not simply wander the countryside randomly spreading apple seeds; rather, his was an organized and efficient operation that guaranteed the apple trees of the east would make the trip west with the American pioneers.

Simple, humble, and pious, Johnny Appleseed became a beloved and respected figure across Ohio and Indiana. The settlers of the early 1800s welcomed him warmly into their homes; but, preferring to live independently outdoors, he declined their offers and went on his way, dressed always in the simple coffee sack and distinctive tin hat. The Native Americans of the area embraced Johnny Appleseed; for in addition to apple seeds, he scattered the seeds of many medicinal plants—pennyroyal, catnip, hoarhound, rattlesnake weed, and others—throughout the forests. As he carried out his unusual mission, Chapman demonstrated a respect for the natural world and a knowledge of its potential powers that was uncommon in his day. This won him the approval of the native people, who regarded him as a man of great healing power.

In all the legends about Johnny Appleseed passed down through the years—by word of mouth and in the works of poets and story-tellers—there is nothing but praise and admiration recorded for this simple man. Ohio legend tells that during the War of 1812, Chapman traveled on foot from village to village warning settlers of coming trouble and saving them from attack. Stories abound of his extraordinary kindness to children and all living creatures; one often repeated legend tells of how all his life he deeply regretted the killing of a rattlesnake that had bitten him. He was also known to have been a devout Christian, eager to read from the Bible or the works of Emanuel Swedenborg to anyone who would listen. One story tells of a minister rhetorically asking his congregation "Where is the man who, like the primitive Christian, walks toward heaven barefoot and clad in sackcloth?" Rising from the back of the congregation, dressed in his usual attire, Johnny Appleseed is said to have answered, "Here is a primitive Christian!" By all accounts, John Chapman was just that—a man who rejected all the material comforts of the world and lived his life guided by faith and a deep love for nature and his fellow Americans.

For most of the early years of the nineteenth century, Johnny Appleseed planted and distributed his apple trees in and around Ashland County, Ohio. During the 1840s, he began to extend his nurseries into the new settlements in Indiana. It was there, near Fort Wayne, that he died in 1847, at the home of a settler who had taken him in after he fell ill on a trip to an outlying nursery. John Chapman left the earth beloved by all who had come into contact with him. A monument to him and other pioneers stands in Ashland County, Ohio; but the greatest monument stands in the form of countless apple trees throughout Ohio and Indiana and in the legends that praise the man who lived a life of humility and simplicity, a man who saw himself not as a master of the natural world but as a responsible, caring part of it.

THE PLANTING OF THE APPLE TREE

William Cullen Bryant

Come, let us plant the apple tree,
Cleave the tough greensward with the spade;
Wide let its hollow bed be made;
There gently lay the roots, and there
Sift the dark mold with kindly care
And press it o'er them tenderly
As, round the sleeping infant's feet,
We softly fold the cradle-sheet:
So plant we the apple tree.

What plant we in this apple tree?
Buds, which the breath of summer days
Shall lengthen into leafy sprays;
Boughs where the thrush, with crimson breast,
Shall haunt and sing and hide her nest;

We plant upon the sunny lea
A shadow for the noontide hour,
A shelter from the summer shower,
When we plant the apple tree.

What plant we in this apple tree?
Sweets for a hundred flowery springs
To load the May wind's restless wings
When from the orchard-row he pours
Its fragrance through our open doors,
A world of blossoms for the bee,
Flowers for the sick girl's silent room,
For the glad infant sprigs of bloom,
We plant with the apple tree.

What plant we in this apple tree?
Fruits that shall swell in sunny June
And redden in the August noon
And drop, when gentle airs come by
That fan the blue September sky,
While children come with cries of glee
And seek them where the fragrant grass
Betrays their bed to those who pass
At the foot of the apple tree.

And when, above this apple tree,
The winter stars are quivering bright
And winds go howling through the night,
Girls, whose young eyes o'erflow with mirth,
Shall peel its fruit by cottage-hearth;
And guests in prouder homes shall see,
Heaped with the grape of Cintra's vine
And golden orange of the line,
The fruit of the apple tree.

The fruitage of this apple tree
Under our flag of stripe and star
Shall sail to coasts that lie afar,
Where men shall wonder at the view
And ask in what fair groves they grew;
And sojourners beyond the sea
Shall think of childhood's careless day
And long, long hours of summer play
In the shade of the apple tree.

Each year shall give this apple tree
A broader flush of roseate bloom,
A deeper maze of verdurous gloom,
And loosen, when the frost-clouds lower,
The crisp, brown leaves in thicker shower.
The years shall come and pass, but we
Shall hear no longer, where we lie,
The summer's songs, the autumn's sigh,
In the boughs of the apple tree.

And time shall waste this apple tree.
Oh, when its aged branches throw
Thin shadows on the ground below,
Shall fraud and force and iron will
Oppress the weak and helpless still?
What shall the tasks of mercy be
Amid the toils, the strifes, the tears
Of those who live when length of years
Is wasting this little apple tree?

"Who planted this old apple tree?"
The children of that distant day
Thus to some aged man shall say;
And, gazing on its mossy stem,
The gray-haired man shall answer them:
"A poet of the land was he,
Born in the rude but good old times;
'Tis said he made some quaint old rhymes,
On planting the apple tree."

FROM THE APPLE BARREL. Fennville, Michigan. Arthur Griggs/Jessie Walker Associates

A Farmer Speaks

Georgia B. Adams

The honey-colored rolling hills
Wave with ripened wheat.
Potato harvest has begun;
I'm in the tractor's seat.

The bands of black soil in the fields
When harvesting is done
Give earnest thanks to God above
For mingled rain and sun.

The corn shock sentinels on guard
In fields with pumpkins strewn
Salute the scarecrow quite forlorn
Beneath a silver moon.

The twisting lane to our farmhouse
Weaves through the aspens tall;
Their leaves like golden shillings dance
To winds of early fall.

Another summer's come and gone!
The silo testifies,
Though mutely, that God's goodness reigns
In earth, in sea, and skies!

GOLDEN FIELD OF GRAIN
Snohomish County, Washington
Ed Cooper Photography

BOUNTIFUL HARVEST

Wava Petersen

The grain in the fields is in season;
The time for the reaping is here;
The golden heads wait ripe and ready
For the harvester's hand to appear.

The stalks stand tall, straight, and sturdy;
Their heads are full and mature;
There is promise of bountiful harvest,
A high-yield crop clean and pure.

The beautiful, golden-ripe product,
As it stands in full-fruited glory,
Tells of a farmer's hard labor—
There's a hint of love in its story.

May our soul-crop look just as pleasing
To the great Master Farmer above;
May we all stand ready for harvest
When He comes with His sickle of love.

Handmade Heirloom

Mary Skarmeas

THE SEVEN DWARFS AS APPLE HEAD DOLLS. Photograph by Ralph Luedtke.

APPLE HEAD DOLLS

Dolls are a cherished part of American childhood. The earliest examples of toy dolls were found in ancient Egypt, Greece, and Rome and were created out of clay, wood, or even linen fabric stuffed with papyrus. As time went on, doll making became increasingly more sophisticated and more diversified. Through all the evolutions and innovations in commercial doll making, however, the art of the handcrafted doll has changed little, relying often on the basic, natural materials and the devotion and imagination of the crafter. In America, handmade dolls have ranged from the simple corn husk variety to the more complex fabric dolls, sewn and stuffed with precision. Doll making today offers the opportunity for a unique, traditional hobby. A handmade doll can be a unique expression of one's own personality or a truly personalized gift. It can carry on a family tradition begun long ago, or begin a new one to be passed on through the years.

One particularly charming, and distinctly American, handmade doll is the apple head doll. Its origins are uncertain. Some claim that American

settlers learned the craft from the Iroquois people; others insist that the skills were brought from European villages. While both assertions may be true, the fact remains that the craft has become a cherished part of American folk art tradition.

The most dazzling feature of the apple head doll is, of course, the head itself, a beautiful, wrinkled face that with practice and patience can take on a remarkably human expression. For the head, firm, under-ripe, crisp apples are best. Some doll makers recommend Jonathans, Winesaps, or Cortlands, which retain their color well. The Macintosh, soft and moist, is unsuitable for drying, but a Golden Delicious can work well. Ask at your local orchard for a variety that suits your purpose.

To begin, peel the apple completely and remove the stem. Prepare the apple with a rinse in cold water and let it air dry for a few minutes. The next step is the most fun *and* the most challenging: carving the features. This is where your own personal style will reveal itself. A few well placed slits in the meat of the apple—one for a mouth, bordered by crescent shaped slits for dimples; one for the nose, a simple vertical line; and two more for the eyes—will result in a soft-featured face. To achieve a face with a more chiseled look, carefully carve away small pieces of apple for each feature: cut a slash for the cheekbone and remove a small piece of the flesh along with the cut; cut a horizontal slash for the mouth and remove some of the apple to show depth; carve out sockets for deep-set eyes. Don't forget to chisel out a chin and a pair of eyebrows. When you've completed carving the features of your apple head doll, soak the head in vinegar or lemon juice for about fifteen minutes if you don't want the features to darken. A whole clove can be pushed into the center of each eye slit to create an eyeball, which can later be embellished with a dab of paint.

Push a wire or a wooden skewer through the core of the carved apple, leaving enough below the apple for hanging during the drying process and to attach to the body later. Attach string to the wire or skewer and hang the head in an airy spot out of the sun to dry. Let the head dry for three to four weeks,

gently molding the features with your fingertips or an orange stick at least every two or three days to achieve just the look you want. As the head dries, it becomes more and more human-like in appearance, and the personality of the doll will emerge. Some doll makers choose to seal the dried heads with varnish while others prefer the natural look. Wood putty works well for sealing any cavities in the top and bottom of the head. When the face is complete and its expression revealed, you can proceed with an appropriate body.

The body of an apple head doll can vary from simple wire shaped into arms and legs and draped with colorful calico to a carefully cut, stitched, and stuffed fabric doll body with custom-made clothes. A simple rag doll will do, as will one made from wood, corn husks, and almost anything else that suits your creative eye. Do make sure that the body allows for the head to be securely attached with wire. One benefit of the simple wire and fabric body is that it can be posed to sit on the mantel, perch on a corner shelf, or stand inside a display cabinet.

Creating apple head dolls is a craft that demands a willingness to experiment. A book may help, but the best way is to start with a whole selection of apples and hope for the best. Only practice and patience will produce the right touch, and even then, each apple turns out differently, and each face develops its own special personality.

Apple head dolls are not playthings but unique, colorful folk art for the home. There is something distinctly "old-fashioned" about a whimsical apple head doll—something of the crispness of fall air, the warmth of the fireplace, and the comforts of home and family. As apples fill the bins at roadside stands and the shelves of your local market this fall, put a few aside and try your hand at this fascinating form of the ancient craft of doll making.

Mary Skarmeas lives in Danvers, Massachusetts, and is studying for her bachelor's degree in English at Suffolk University. Mother of four and grandmother of one, Mary loves all crafts, especially knitting.

Old Time Apples

Dan A. Hoover

When summer sun like polished brass
    Cured clover hay in scorching air,
We climbed our Early Harvest trees
    For mellow apples lurking there

Or spliced our fish poles in a plan
    To knock the striped Astrakhan;
Yellow Transparent lured us too
    For fruit-bait goodness overdue.

On August noons, wheat-threshing crews
    Lay resting under maple shade;

We found the streaked Sheepnose ripe
    And filled straw hats with every raid.

With autumn days of bronze and gold,
    As cobwebs floated on the breeze,
A host of old-time favorites bowed
    The boughs of family-orchard trees.

Wolf River's heavy, flattened fruit,
    The Duchess and Bellflower's spice,
Red Wealthy's mealy, tempting bite
    Made apple-eating paradise.

Now new kinds ship and rarely bruise
    To sparkle bright on Produce Row
But lack the subtle flavor thrills
    Of orchard tastes we used to know.

The Right Answer

Margaret Rorke

A giant check mark, southward bound,
Has crossed the sunset sky;
A feathered fork with honking sound
Has solemnly passed by
As though a teacher, left of hand,
Had caught some grave mistake—
Not born of earth, you understand,
But such as clouds can make.
The question we cannot detect.
The answer we can't scoff.
It may be just that Someone checked
Another summer off.

Thanksgiving

Raymond Orner

We're thankful for our heritage
We never want to lose
And for a nation where we're free
To worship as we choose.

We're thankful for equality
In spite of race or creed
And for the great abundance of
The things we daily need.

We're thankful for the open door
That leads to greater things.
We lift our hearts to God in joy;
His praises do we sing.

For wooded hills and fruited plains
And friends along the way,
We give our thanks to God above
On this Thanksgiving Day.

TRAVELER'S
Diary

Lisa C. Thompson

IMMIGRATION STATION, MAIN BUILDING. Ellis Island, New York, New York. Superstock Photograph.

ELLIS ISLAND IMMIGRATION MUSEUM
Ellis Island, New York

Warmed by the glow of Lady Liberty's raised torch just yards away in the New York Harbor, the Ellis Island Immigration Museum stands as a tribute to the millions of immigrants who passed through its doors in their quest for a new life. The museum occupies the renovated Main Building of the most famous Immigration Station in the world, where, between 1892 and 1954, more than twelve million immigrants were processed and granted freedom in America. More than forty percent of all living Americans today can trace their own ancestry to immigrants who came through Ellis Island. The

stories of these ancestors, the individual immigrants, are told in the museum through photographs, letters, displays of their possessions, and oral narratives from actual immigrants themselves.

I disembark the crowded ferry to Ellis Island with the other visitors and enter the Great Hall of the main building much in the same way my ancestors did years ago. It was here that the immigrants began the tedious process of being inspected and questioned and sometimes marked with chalk for further examination. (Wily immigrants turned their coats inside out to hide the dreaded chalk marks.) With the number of visitors to the museum sometimes reaching ten to fifteen thousand in a single day, the effect of walking through the hall feels eerily similar to what those tired travelers must have felt and heard as they struggled to hear the important instructions echoing throughout the huge room.

As I strain to hear the tour guide, I can hear a group of people walking up the stairs behind me speaking in a language I do not immediately recognize, yet another reminder of what the immigrants experienced. We all walk together through the many rooms of the second floor. Surrounding the great hall, an exhibit entitled "Through America's Gate" includes a flowchart of the steps to freedom that the immigrants dutifully followed and also sound recordings of their reminiscences. "Peak Immigration Years," also on the second floor, details the whole experience of an immigrant leaving his or her homeland, often for the first time. Again, I find myself wondering about my own ancestors. Did they flee starvation during the devastating potato famine in Ireland, as so many did during the 1840s? Were they in search of religious freedom or economic prosperity? Why did they come to America?

THE JOURNEY TO FREEDOM. California Museum of Photography, Keystone-Mast Collection, University of California, Riverside.

On the third floor at the "Treasures from Home" exhibit, we learn about the personal lives of some of the immigrants. We see their photographs, their letters, and even some of their personal artifacts—a battered trunk, a wooden hatbox, a passport. Two additional exhibits also occupy the third floor, "Ellis Island Chronicles" and "Silent Voices."

I feel a bit unsteady on this small tract of land when I learn at the "Ellis Island Chronicles" exhibit that it was once three acres of mud barely rising above sea level, home only to gulls and oysters. Landfill from New York City subway tunnels helped to build up the island into something more substantial. I learn of the great fire in 1897 which destroyed every building on Ellis Island but, thankfully, killed no one. I read about how President Lyndon B. Johnson, in 1965, granted Ellis Island landmark status as a part of the State of Liberty National Monument, with the National Park Service as its caretaker.

"Silent Voices" depicts the abandoned state of Ellis Island from the time the Immigration Station was closed in 1954 up to the time of its renovation during the 1980s. A deserted and lonely place, Ellis Island was neglected until a resurging interest in ethnic heritage among many Americans persuaded the government to renovate. Eight years and $156 million later, the Ellis Island Immigration Museum opened in 1990.

Before I leave the Main Building, I quietly slip into a comfortable seat in one of the two theaters to view the film *Island of Hope/Island of Tears* by the Oscar-winning filmmaker Charles Guggenheim. Narrated by actor Gene Hackman, the film brings to life the emotions of the immigrants. We see their faces and hear their stories. We sense their courage and fierce determination to reach freedom.

At the film's conclusion, I wander outside to walk along the American Immigrant Wall of Honor, which commemorates the names of more than 420,000 individuals and families that immigrated through Ellis Island. Visitors are stopping at points along the wall to photograph the names of their family members. I see the names of several Thompsons, but I do not know them. Perhaps they are distant relatives, removed from me by the expanses of time. Despite my lack of connection to any specific name on the wall or photograph in the museum, I do feel connected to these immigrants. I share their deep pride in calling myself an American, and I feel the joy and thanksgiving they felt on the day they were granted freedom.

Autumn Song

Arlette Lees Baker

When autumn bites the brittle air,
We raid the cedar chest
For patchwork quilts and fluffy downs
To line our winter nest.

70

We gather chestnuts in the woods
    To roast before the snows
And ball our scarlet yarn for socks
    To toast our winter toes.

We bunch our beds beneath the beams
    And cut a length of log
And share the crackling woodbox warmth
    With cat and mouse and dog.

We save a sad, sweet memory
    For summers burning bright
Then cuddle up with cocoa cups
    To greet the frosty night.

From My Garden Journal

by Deana Deck

HEATHER

A few years back I vacationed in Ireland, and one of the things I was greatly looking forward to was the sight of the fabled "heather on the hill." I'm sure I was influenced by subliminal images of the tragic Heathcliff, lamenting the love of his life, skulking through the heather and gorse as he haunted the desolate moors surrounding Wuthering Heights. Although Heathcliff's story was set in England, his name gives a clue to the habitat of these tough little plants. Throughout the British Isles, both the heath and the heather grow along rocky cliff tops in sheltered crevices. Both are similar in appearance, require similar growing conditions, and are usually referred to as "heather" by florists. The plant that is commonly sold as Mediterranean heather is actually a heath and does a little bit better in hot climates than does true heather.

But I was looking for Scotch heather (*Calluna vulgaris*), and during my leisurely drive across Ireland from Dublin to Galway, I began to doubt its existence in that part of the world. I saw no moors, only vast, green, boulder-studded fields which had been neatly clipped to the ground by the ubiquitous sheep. It wasn't until I was nearing the spectacular Cliffs of Moher that I finally caught a glimpse of a wild and barren stretch of boggy soil covered with a carpet of rose-tinted native heather.

It was my luck to be traveling in September, which is the season heather blooms most profusely; and although I was unaware of it at the time, the reason I didn't spot any heather in my trip across the rich farmland of central Ireland was that the plant actually prefers a lean, porous, acidic soil of pH 6.0 or lower, in which very little else will grow. It also doesn't do well in windswept vistas because it intensely dislikes wind. It will, however, do quite well when sheltered in the lee of a rising hill or near a crumbling stone wall or a rocky outcropping, all of which are abundant in the part of Ireland where I finally caught sight of it.

The kind of heather I yearned to glimpse is the one most familiar to gardeners, and it grows throughout Europe as abundantly as in Scotland. It is not a difficult plant to grow, and if you are in the midst of holiday decorating, you might pause to consider it as an addition to your garden for next spring. Heather in containers makes a lovely evergreen addition to holiday decor, and when dried, the fern-like foliage and colorful blooms are attractive in floral arrangements and impart a musky, sweet scent to the room. Sprigs of fresh-cut heather mixed with cinnamon-scented white cushion chrysanthemums can provide a handsome variation on the traditional Thanksgiving arrangement of football mums and autumn leaves.

Although usually considered a rose-hued bloomer, heather is available in a variety of colors. Scotch heather blooms in shades of varying intensity from white through pink to red. *Calluna alba* produces white blooms in August and September, and *Calluna aurea* features golden yellow leaves which produce crimson flowers from July to October.

For fresh-cut blooms, consider *Calluna foxi* "H. E. Beale," a two-inch plant with double, soft rose-hued flowers in bloom from September to November. Another late bloomer is the *Calluna searlei,* a two-foot plant with silvery foliage that produces white blooms from September to November.

Heather has a reputation for being difficult to grow in the garden, but that is only true if you are unaware of its requirements. It does best in acid, rather moist soil and in late winter benefits from some light shade. It is hardy to most of the United States, even as far north as southern North Dakota and southern Maine. For colder climates, heather can be easily grown in containers, which also afford more control over soil moisture and acidity.

Heather actually performs better in poor soil than in a rich garden environment,

My heather dried best when I let it stand in water and dry out very slowly. It was less brittle and easier to work with.

which makes it ideal for rock gardens, sandy banks, roadsides, and other challenging spots where little else performs well. In rich soil, the plant tends to grow unkempt and leggy, producing unattractive flopping branches. It is highly attractive in beds of dwarf conifers and in bold drifts in front of a sunny border of green shrubbery. Also, heather's compact growth habit makes it well suited for container growing.

Heather also makes an attractive ground cover, with evergreen foliage available in gold, orange, bronze, gray-green, and green. To keep it thick and low-growing, it's best to prune it in late winter or very early spring when it has plenty of time to leaf out and thicken into a dense mat. It's not a good idea to wait until summer for this type of pruning because the plants will not have time to harden off before killing frosts occur and new growth is badly damaged.

Heather is remarkably simple to dry. Unlike many plants, it needs to be dried upright rather than by hanging in order for the blooms to maintain a natural appearance. Heather can also be allowed to dry out slowly in water as part of an arrangement and seems to do best when dried in this fashion. The stems become less brittle, and it is more easily added to other arrangements or holiday wreaths.

Deana Deck lives in Nashville, Tennessee, where her garden column is a regular feature in The Tennessean.

The Old Oak Tree

Nora M. Bozeman

The seasoned oak tree stood alone.
Her limbs were bare and weather-blown;
Her massive trunk was cracked and dry;
On windy days she seemed to sigh.

The old oak tree will always be
Standing there unbendingly;
To look at her you would not know
She reached one hundred—years ago.

She stands tall, beyond compare,
In majestic beauty rare;
I look at her, and I can see
Victorious is the old oak tree.

Leaves of Late Autumn

Wilma Black

They lie upon the walk beneath my feet,
The color faded now to dim and muted tone
Like fragile silks worn long ago and laid away,
Brittle to touch and faintly redolent

Inside border. ACER RUBRUM. Red Maple in Missouri. Gay Bumgarner Photography

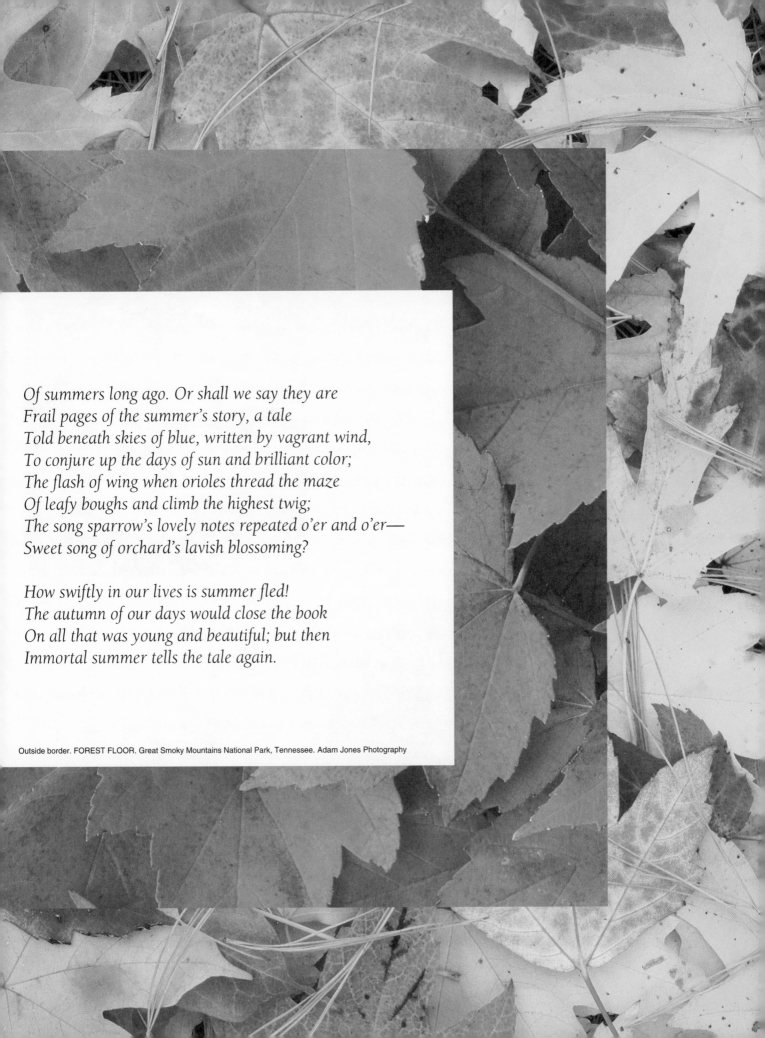

Of summers long ago. Or shall we say they are
Frail pages of the summer's story, a tale
Told beneath skies of blue, written by vagrant wind,
To conjure up the days of sun and brilliant color;
The flash of wing when orioles thread the maze
Of leafy boughs and climb the highest twig;
The song sparrow's lovely notes repeated o'er and o'er—
Sweet song of orchard's lavish blossoming?

How swiftly in our lives is summer fled!
The autumn of our days would close the book
On all that was young and beautiful; but then
Immortal summer tells the tale again.

Outside border. FOREST FLOOR. Great Smoky Mountains National Park, Tennessee. Adam Jones Photography

Readers' Forum

Meet Our Ideals Readers and Their Families

FAITH GREEN of Orange, Massachusetts, sent us this snapshot of her grandchildren, Robin, eight years old, and Colton, seven. Faith made the costumes for a Halloween party the children were attending at school, and they also wore them later for trick-or-treating. Robin and Colton recently moved to Henderson, Nevada, with their mother, Carrie Hannula. Faith hasn't yet ventured out West for a visit but hopes to soon.

In addition to sewing Faith enjoys painting with acrylics, wood-cutting, and gardening. Each summer she works at a country inn in New Hampshire tending the perennial flower beds.

Faith has been subscribing to *Ideals* for more than twenty years and enjoys her subscription very much.

ROSS AND MILDRED WATTS of Palmyra, Pennsylvania, feed and watch over the most popular squirrel in the neighborhood—a beautiful albino with pink eyes. Mildred enjoys photography as a hobby and has taken several shots of the well-fed squirrel.

Sharing a love of the outdoors, the Watts enjoy camping. Ross, a retired principal, is now mayor of Palmyra; and when he's not working or camping, he loves to be out on the golf course.

The Watts have been subscribing to *Ideals* for many years; Mildred got her first subscription as a Christmas present from the church superintendent for helping out in the church nursery.

During this Thanksgiving season, Mildred says she has much to be thankful for including good health, her family (they have two children and five grandchildren), and the beauties of the earth.

H. BIRDINE BURNETT of Wolfeboro, New Hampshire, sent us the above photograph of the sun setting on Lake Winnipesaukee, which is right outside her window. Birdine has lived right on the lake for the past fifteen years. She says the sunset is often quite beautiful, but this particular one inspired her to write the following poem:

Day's End

As I sit and watch the sunsets,
As evening closes in,
I think of the "brush" of our Master
With His purples, golds, and His pinks.
No man could accomplish this ever,
No matter how young or how old.
What a wonderful way to close my day,
With my Master, His sunset, and me.

Thank you Faith Green, Ross and Mildred Watts, and Birdine Burnett for sharing with *Ideals* this Thanksgiving. We hope to hear from other readers who would like to share photos and stories with the *Ideals* family. Please include a self-addressed, stamped envelope if you would like the photos returned. Keep your original photographs for safekeeping and send duplicate photos along with your name, address, and telephone number to:

Readers' Forum
Ideals Publications Inc.
P.O. Box 148000
Nashville, TN 37214-8000

Publisher, Patricia A. Pingry
Editor, Lisa C. Thompson
Art Director, Patrick McRae
Copy Editor, Laura Matter
Editorial Assistant, Crystal Edison
Contributing Editors, Lansing Christman, Deana Deck, Russ Flint, Pamela Kennedy, Mary Skarmeas, Nancy Skarmeas

ACKNOWLEDGMENTS

THANKSGIVING by May Allread Baker taken from *WILLOW BROOK FARM* by May Allread Baker. Copyright 1946, Brethren Publishing House. Used by permission. APPLES RIPE FOR EATING from *THE PASSING THRONG* by Edgar Guest, copyright ©1923 by the Reilly & Lee Co., used by permission of the author's estate. AUTUMN TAPESTRY from *FLOWERS OF FRIENDSHIP* by Patience Strong, first published by Frederick Muller Ltd. in 1955, reproduced by permission of Rupert Crew Limited. NOVEMBER by Gladys Taber from *THE STILLMEADOW ROAD* by Gladys Taber, copyright 1959, 1960, 1962, by Gladys Taber. Copyright renewed ©1990 by Constance Taber Colby. Reprinted by permission of Brandt & Brandt Literary Agents, Inc. Our sincere thanks to the following authors whom we were unable to contact: Gertrude Ryder Bennett for HARVEST FIELD; George Z. Keller for WE GIVE THANKS; Raymond Orner for THANKSGIVING; Florence Ray for THE FIRST THANKSGIVING DAY; and Elizabeth McFerren Youtz for MOUNTAIN MUSIC.

GIVE A GIFT FROM IDEALS THIS CHRISTMAS

**THE BEST
OF IDEALS**
Order #40377A

**REMEMBER
WHEN**
Order #40458A

**AN AMERICAN
FAMILY TREASURY**
Order #40490A

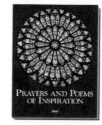

**PRAYERS AND POEMS
OF INSPIRATION**
Order #40474A

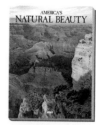

**AMERICA'S
NATURAL BEAUTY**
Order #40482A

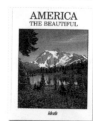

**AMERICA THE
BEAUTIFUL**
Order #10710AA

**BACKROADS
OF AMERICA**
Order #40369A

**CAROLS OF
CHRISTMAS**
Order #40547A

**50th ANNIVERSARY
COLLECTOR'S EDITION**
Order #11261A

5-PACK
Order #07806A

**AMERICA THE
BEAUTIFUL
1995 PERSONAL
CALENDAR**
Order #40601A

Enjoy a different picture of
our impressive country
each week in this inspiring,
week-at-a-glance calendar.

**OUR
PRESIDENTS**
Order #1127XA

5-PACK W/ENVELOPES
Order #07807A

**PATRIOTIC
3-PACK**
Order #07802A

Celebrate the triumphs of
America through song, verse,
prose, and photography. Each
volume in this set celebrates
the patriotic spirit that
makes our nation great.

PATRIOTIC 3-PACK	#07802A
INDIVIDUAL ORDERS:	
OUR AMERICA	#10990A
5-PACK W/ENVELOPES	#07653A
HEAR AMERICA SINGING	#11172A
5-PACK W/ENVELOPES	#07778A
THE STORY OF AMERICA	#11059A
5-PACK W/ENVELOPES	#07672A

**IDEALS
FRIENDSHIP**
Order #11202A

5-PACK W/ENVELOPES
#07808A

**IDEALS
CHRISTMAS**
Order #11229A

5-PACK W/ENVELOPES
Order #07809A

**IDEALS
BINDER**
Order #D10713

**IDEALS
SLIPCASE**
Order #10796

Sturdy construction protects one year of *Ideals*
and makes favorite volumes easy to locate.

BINDER	#D10713
SLIPCASE	#10796